THE LITTLE BOOK OF
THAILAND

Photography and words
Julian Bound

INTRODUCTION

The Eastern Coast of Koh Samui, Thailand

Formally recognised as Siam until 1939, and again from 1945 to 1949, The Kingdom of Thailand is located in the centre of the Indochinese Peninsula where its 76 provinces is home to over 66 million people.

Known for its tropical beaches, ornate Buddhist temples and ancient ruins, Thailand's capital Bangkok combines both the traditional and the new with its cityscape of ultramodern buildings sitting effortlessly beside canal side communities and tranquil riverside temples. 300miles/480km north of Bangkok, the city of Chiang Mai retains Thailand's cultural heritage, its Old City's moat and walled area holding a multitude of elaborate Buddhist temples.

Further south on Thailand's eastern coast line, the island of Koh Samui and its palm-fringed beaches, coconut groves and mountainous rainforest is host to the golden Buddha statue of Wat Phra Yai temple, who standing at 12m/39ft overlooks the warm waters of the Gulf of Thailand.

STONE BUDDHA HEAD
AYUTTHAYA HISTORICAL PARK

PREPARING FOR MEDITATION
WAT CHEDI LUAN, CHIANG MAI

MONK OF THE BIG BUDDHA TEMPLE
WAT PHRA YAI, KOH SAMUI

BUDDHIST NUN OF WAT CHANA SONGKRAM
BANG LAMPHU, BANGKOK
10

BUDDHIST NUN OF WAT CHANA SONGKRAM
BANG LAMPHU, BANGKOK

WAT CHANA SONGKRAM
BANG LAMPHU, BANGKOK

BUDDHIST MONK OF WAT CHANA SONGKRAM
BANG LAMPHU, BANGKOK

THE BACK STREETS OF BANG LAMPHU
BANG LAMPHU, BANGKOK

STREET VENDOR OF BANG LAMPHU
BANG LAMPHU, BANGKOK

STREET FOOD VENDOR OF BANG LAMPHU
BANG LAMPHU, BANGKOK

HAT SELLER OF YAOWARAT MARKET
CHINATOWN, BANGKOK

STREET VENDOR OF PRATUNAM MARKETS
PRATUNAM, BANGKOK

STREET FOOD SELLER
KHAO SAN ROAD, BANGKOK

STONE BUDDHA STATUE
AYUTTHAYA HISTORICAL PARK

BUDDHA AND STUPA
AYUTTHAYA HISTORICAL PARK

SUKHOTHAI
SUKHOTHAI HISTORICAL PARK

PHRA POOD DAI
SUKHOTHAI HISTORICAL PARK

BUDDHA STATUES
WAT PHO, BANGKOK

PRAYERS IN WAT CHANA SONGKRAM
BANG LAMPHU, BANGKOK

GOLDEN BUDDHA
WAT PHO, BANGKOK

BUDDHA STATUE
WAT PHO, BANGKOK

WAT CHANA SONGKRAM
BANG LAMPHU, BANGKOK

MONKS OF WAT CHANA SONGKRAM
BANG LAMPHU, BANGKOK

MONK OF SUKHOTHAI
SUKHOTHAI

MONK OF SUKHOTHAI
SUKHOTHAI

WAT CHANA SONGKRAM
BANG LAMPHU, BANGKOK

ELDERLY MONK OF AYUTTHAYA
AYUTTHAYA HISTORICAL PARK

About The Author

Born in the UK, Julian Bound is a documentary photographer, film maker and author. Featured on the BBC news, National Geographic and in the international press, his work focuses on the social documentary of world culture, religion and traditions, spending time studying meditation with the Buddhist monks of Tibet and Northern Thailand and with spiritual teachers of India's Himalaya region.

His photography work includes documenting the child soldiers of the Burmese Karen National Liberation Army, the Arab Spring of 2011, Cairo, Egypt, and the Thailand political uprisings of 2009 and 2014 in Bangkok.

With portraiture of His Holiness the 14th Dalai Lama, Julian has photographed the Tibetan refugee camps of Nepal and India. His other projects include the road working gypsies of India, the Dharavi slums of Mumbai, the rail track slums of Jakarta and the sulphur miners at work in the active volcanoes of Eastern Java, Indonesia.

Present for the Nepal earthquakes of 2015, he documented the disaster whilst working as an emergency deployment photographer for various NGO and international embassies in conjunction with the United Nations.

ALSO BY THE AUTHOR

THE LITTLE BOOK OF
TIBET

A PHOTOGRAPHIC JOURNEY
PHOTOGRAPHY AND WORDS
JULIAN BOUND

THE LITTLE BOOK OF
NEPAL

A PHOTOGRAPHIC JOURNEY
PHOTOGRAPHY AND WORDS
JULIAN BOUND

THE LITTLE BOOK OF
BHUTAN

A PHOTOGRAPHIC JOURNEY
PHOTOGRAPHY AND WORDS
JULIAN BOUND

THE LITTLE BOOK OF
JAPAN

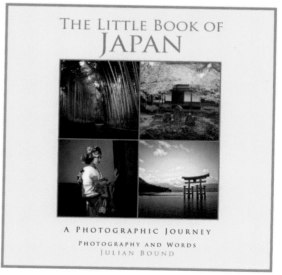

A PHOTOGRAPHIC JOURNEY
PHOTOGRAPHY AND WORDS
JULIAN BOUND

From National Geographic contributer and documentary photographer Julian Bound, a collection of books exploring the landscapes, traditions, culture and people of Tibet, Nepal, Bhutan and Japan in colour and black and white.

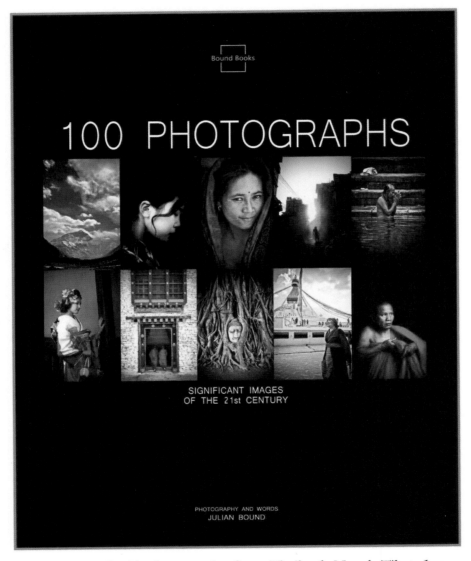

A collection of 100 photographs from Thailand, Nepal, Tibet, Japan, India, Bhutan, Cambodia, Laos, Indonesia, Myanmar and England, by National Geographic photography contributor Julian Bound.

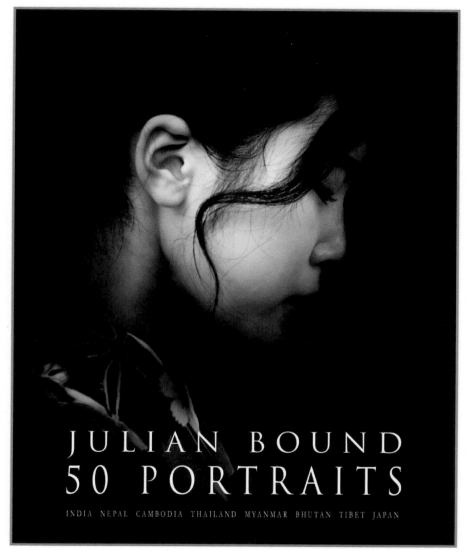

JULIAN BOUND
50 PORTRAITS

INDIA NEPAL CAMBODIA THAILAND MYANMAR BHUTAN TIBET JAPAN

By National Geographic contributer and award winning documentary photographer Julian Bound, a collection of portraiture work taken in India, Nepal, Cambodia, Thailand, Myanmar, Bhutan, Tibet and Japan.

Printed in Great Britain
by Amazon